ENERGY CRISIS

Philippa Holloway is an author and academic, teaching Creative Writing at Staffordshire University. Her debut novel, *The Half-life of Snails,* has achieved critical acclaim and was longlisted for the RSL Ondaatje Prize. Her short fiction/non-fiction is published internationally. She has been recognized in literary awards including the Rhys Davies Short Story Prize and the Writers & Artists Working Class Writer's Prize. She is the co-curator of a global writing project responding to the pandemic and the collection *100 Words of Solitude: Global Voices in Lockdown 2020* (Rare Swan Press), and is currently co-authoring a textbook on Creative Writing and the Anthropocene. Twitter/Instagram: @thejackdawspen

Also by Philippa Holloway

The Half-life of Snails   (Parthian, 2022)

100 Words of Solitude (co-editor)   (Rare Swan Press, 2021)

The Message   (Nightjar Press, 2018)

Energy Crisis:
Memoir of Summer

Philippa Holloway

Broken Sleep Books

ISBN: 978-1-915760-91-3

Cover designed by Aaron Kent

Edited by Cathleen Allyn Conway

Typeset by Aaron Kent

Broken Sleep Books Ltd   Broken Sleep Books Ltd
Rhydwen   Fair View
Talgarreg   St Georges Road
Ceredigion   Cornwall
SA44 4HB   PL26 7YH

Contents

In crisis 7

Solar Power 9

Wind Power 17

Tidal Power 27

Nuclear Power 35

Fossil Fuel 41

Will Power 45

Notes and Acknowledgements 51

In crisis

Imagine me, for a moment, clinging to a rock face. Legs in the shade of the rising shoulder of Tryfan on the other side of the gully, head illuminated by early September sunshine. My hair, sticking out in squirrel tufts from beneath the helmet, is the colour of leaves in the autumn.

But the trees around here haven't quite used up the sun yet, are still in their green dresses and hats. I'm not dressed for climbing: jeans, baseball shoes, a top that could spill my cleavage unless I maintain a suitable posture. But here I am, 30 feet up in the air, clinging with bone-pale fingers to the smallest cracks and fissures, my aching toes pushing hard into a crevice of solid, ancient stone.

I am moss.

I am lichen.

I am the trembling tree rooted in the memory of dirt beside me.

And I am tired.

I was tired before I started. I was tired watching the others as they skittered up like lizards on hot rock, arms and legs wide and reaching for muscle-tearing holds before spinning down like spiders with arms and legs wide in triumph.

I sat on a smooth, cold stone at the bottom, feeling my own weight in stillness, every joint a dull and rusty ache, deciding not to even try. But here I am.

Imagine me clinging to the rock face, then leave me there a while.

Don't worry, I won't fall and crack my skull like a bird's lost egg on the rocks below. I have a harness and ropes, a helmet to ensure safety.

I'm leaning into the sun-baked roughness of that time-carved wall and not able to move another inch. Leave me there a while.

Solar Power

Summer starts, for me, with dandelions. They erupt after the pale agreeing heads of the daffodils have withered to brown and begun to relent. The roadsides and fields are ablaze with them. They are my favourite flower, and as I drive along the dual carriageways and B-roads that twist colubrine through Gwynedd and Ynys Môn, I am grinning like a kid on a Friday at 3pm. Their magnitude and attitude fuels me. So far it has been what everyone describes as 'unseasonably warm for this time of year', but the Earth doesn't know this and just silently shifts gear and gets on with it without checking a calendar, worrying, or rejoicing. No matter how hot the early sun beats down, the dandelions burn defiantly back; heads upturned, dark green arms spread wide to catch their energy source, turn it into chlorophyll. To grow ever taller.

As I drive past the fields where their gold coin optimism is piled and scattered, I feel compelled to pull over. I want to step through the thorny claws of defensive hedges and roll down the hill as I did as a child, sending millions of things, all legs and wings, into the hazy air and smelling the dark green of crushed leaves and stems beneath me. I think of the sticky white blood that stained my young skin, that made perfect printed *O*s of bitter sap on my clothes, and I want to feel it again – knowing its harsh taste somewhere in my cell memory, knowing how hard it is to wash off, how red the skin goes with the rubbing. Worth it for the tumble, for the letting go…

I want that.

The pure energy of gravity pulling me down the slope, faster and faster, kinetic and absolute and leaving me dizzy and out of breath despite the lack of effort on my part.

Knowing that the destructive path of my rolling body won't stop them, that's part of the joy. Even the strimmers and ride-on mowers the council workers use to decapitate and crush all striving Spring growth can't stop the dandelions. Two, maybe three days after the slaughter, as the severed stalks and dead insects begin to dry out and brown under the weight of the sun, the lights will come back on. One by one, orange and angry and joyful. Their energy is indestructible, their resilience unstoppable.

But mine isn't.

I can't stop and roll in their colourful heat, or collect their rich dark bitter leaves to feed a pet rabbit long since dead – I have an appointment to attend. The clock on the dashboard says I'm early, but not early enough to stop and use up the last dregs of my own energy in a game.

My arm rests on the open window frame of the driver's-side door, bare to the sun bar for the layer of factor-50 sunscreen that is now a daily routine. A smooth, invisible layer of synthetic skin between me and nature, a shield to defy the elements and cut off all communication between the sun and my skin.

Almost all.

My skin is warm, hot even, and I know time will limit my protection. Unlike those brazen dandelions who steal the power and colour and heat of that hanging ball of flame in the sky and turn it into a billion suns of their own, I cover up; smear on my creams and oils to stop its power getting through. UVA and UVB are my mortal enemies. I check each beauty spot and mole punctuating my skin regularly to see if any rays have made it through, if there are any signs of change.

My skin should stay the same colour all year round. Safe. Pale.

Since time began, the sun has been a primary source of energy for all living things on the planet. As I sit in traffic, I can see its shimmering heat reflected above the tin roofs of the cars ahead. I try to think of something that does not demand its radiating gift to survive and thrive. Perhaps within the darkest caves, below the deepest seas, there are creatures more pale than me that don't know what it is to bask in and soak up heat and light.

In fact, I know they are there; I've seen the documentaries and watched in fascinated abjection the footage of their eyeless, rubbery bodies exposed by artificial light and underwater technology. But even these black spaces are part of something bigger; they interact with an ecosystem that does rely on the sun. You only need to look at the faces in town in the slump of a January afternoon to know that sunlight is life.

My skin prickles; sweat glues me to the seat through my shirt.

It's only May and therefore not even summer yet. The fuel light on my dashboard comes on, a bleep to tell me I only have 76 miles to go until the engine stops. I can go to a garage on the way home, pour diesel made from crude oil remnants of ancient forests grown under the same sky above me now into the tank, and power myself home on the carbon memory of the sun.

The car park smells hot and green, windows reflect white light that makes me squint in pain, and as I pass the fuzzy shrub borders, bees and insects vibrate in suckling glee. Every step I take is an effort, like walking through hot, shifting sand. My knees and ankles throb with it.

Inside, the examination room is cool. The thudding turn of the fan syncs with my heartbeat as latex fingers explore my skin for signs of damage, each speckle, freckle and dark mark explored and measured while I think of my mother and the operation last year to excise a lemon-wedge shaped area of tissue with cancer at the core.

Nothing unusual. Keep checking. Wear sunscreen.

What about the fatigue? The aching joints? Could it be vitamin D deficiency? Rickets? I don't eat meat, I don't let the sun close, I keep that second skin of chemicals and cloth between me and its healing, hurting radiation. Could it be I *need* the sun?

I am dismissed with repeated instructions to keep checking, to keep using sunscreen. There is nothing to suggest anything serious. Drink more milk.

Later on, in the middle of summer, I sit in the garden, the toothy outline of Eryri smiling above the tree line. We plant seeds, my son and I. Dig the cool black soil with our hands, breaking great clods of burnt cake earth into fine, sifting soil.

His fingers push punctuation marks into the surface and we drop a seed in each hole like a shard of hope, patting the nutritious earth flat with open palms. Water from the rusty can and then let the sun do the rest.

The packet says two weeks should yield the shoots, but the trees that guard the edge of our property are sucking the sunlight into their widening leaves, chlorophyl coursing and strengthening their outspread arms and filtering the rays into blinking firefly dapples.

After a month, I know the crop is stillborn. The first hopeful shoots starved of light.

Shade is keeping the soil damp, the trees above as thick as thieves and burning green. We give up picking wet slugs off the slimy wall above the cold earth. I sit in the shade, coated in sunscreen, and hold a cup of cooling coffee while my son plays in the park beyond the fence. He is turning brown despite his hat and my regular attacks with the factor-50. He is flourishing. When he gets undressed to shower, his thighs and backside are white as winter.

His metamorphosis started on a school trip to Traeth Bychan, during which my instructions to keep coating his skin in bottled protection were forgotten. That evening I watched his apple cheeks turn into infernos, his back scream pain throughout his tiny body. Sleep came late. He couldn't lie still, couldn't sit or sleep until after-sun was slathered onto his fiery flesh and I lay beside him speaking soft, cool words, blowing on his spine.

I stood at the window afterwards and cursed the sunset's arrogant display of colours on the horizon. Guilt and rage burned my belly. When he turned brown within a few days I cursed the attitude of folk who lie for hours trying to achieve the same result. To look healthy these days is to be burnt.

I look ill.

Pale as a pebble, moon sick and sallow.

A fortnight later, I'm walking among the ones I cursed, their bodies laid on the beach like driftwood. The weather is too good to stay inside. I strip down to my bathing suit and spray protective lotions onto my transparent skin, feel heat flood through my uppermost surfaces and seep up from the hot white sand into the soles of my feet. I step, determined, towards the sea – let the cool water trick me into thinking it's not that hot today, the clouds making the sun wink every now and then. Afterwards I sit and let the sun bake me dry. I can feel heat, but not burning. I try to imagine it feeding me with energy, filling each cell with power and light to boost me into the rest of the month.

Everywhere I look on the journey to and from the sea there are houses wearing solar panel hats, their green credentials on display for all the sky to see. This summer they are storing plenty of electricity and feeding the National Grid. I wonder how long it will last. I feel like I should be energised too. It does that, the sun. Makes everything look bright and fresh, makes you feel like you can do anything, should do everything. So few days are warm enough to swim in a lake, play on a beach, eat outside despite the flies from the water and the neighbour's lawnmower droning over your conversation like a giant wasp, irritating and unavoidable. It lures you outside and tells you to play, swim, run, walk.

But really it saps your strength.

By the end of the day, I can barely drive home.

By evening I realise the sunscreen failed. My back is scarlet with white lines to mark out my folly. I imagine vitamin D soaking into my bones, wait for the pain in my skin to ease the pain in my joints.

It doesn't.

By September that year, some newspapers are rejoicing in the best summer for years, ignoring warnings of climate change, the risks that the sun brings: forest fires, water shortages, mortality in the most vulnerable. Denial is a privilege slowly eroded.

We had one or two days of blissful and blessed rain, remembered as a dream, a godsend, a respite. Despite the sunscreen and sunburn, I've turned beige. My freckles merge across my nose, annex my cheeks. I look 'healthy', or so they say. I'm exhausted from seeking the sun's energy.

My hair looks like its on fire in the last rays over Tryfan.

I can't climb any higher.

Wind Power

I'm woken by the trees tapping pale green fingertips against the bedroom windowpane. They are so close to the house that all I can see when I draw back the drapes is a shifting, surging rustle of greens. Silver birch, tall and slender, stand the closest, willow a few boughs back with its swaying, swirling branches trailing towards the ground. Then buddleia and fir, hiding the houses beyond our garden from view. The heavy rise of redwoods guard the horizon.

The wind is making them sing, a shushing, rushing chorus that gives the impression the house is moving, borne up and away on a frantic journey. I get back into bed and watch the small silver section of sky lighten above the trees' tossing heads from the warmth of a heavy duvet. This morning there is no urgency to rise. The school run and work are on hold for a while. Alarms are not set.

But the world wants to play.

These are days for kite flying, for brisk walks along the beach, watching seagulls fight and fly the invisible force of the air on outstretched wings. I curl into myself, savour the depth of the mattress and imagine the day ahead.

It can't be wasted.

Already the sun is arguing with the wind over who gets to rule. I think a truce will be struck; the wind will lure people out on the sea, yachtsmen and kite surfers, and the sun will make them believe they are safe.

Nothing can go wrong on a bright day like this. The wind will keep a soothing chill to the skin while the sun burns surreptitiously. I am wise to their tricks, will take both sunscreen and a cardigan out with me later.

After dizzying myself watching the rolling treetops for a while, I wrap up in an unnecessary dressing gown and head down to make coffee, take painkillers. The dog is prancing, excited by the rushing of the new leaves beyond the window. She is old, too old to run anymore, but forgets, and chases leaves on the patio, slapping paws down and snapping jaws that would be white with age if they weren't already white by breed. She limps back in, clatters claws across the floor, and flops into a windswept heap, the energy she's stolen from the wind just as quickly sucked away by it.

I wait for caffeine to waken my senses and settle my stomach. I'm hopeful that today I can get out and do something, feel my place in a world bigger than the bed or the sofa or the computer chair. Most days my limited energy resources are consumed by duty; work, the school run and homework, cooking and doing the dishes. Most days all I have left is an hour in front of the TV, watching pretend people achieve pretend goals before I collapse into pretend dreams. Today is a day off – I'm going to ignore the chores and take my son out, walk into the wind and then turn, let it push me home.

I pack sandwiches, snacks and drinks, a football, buckets and spades. What's the point of living by the sea if you only see the beach on the commute to work? We load into the car and I pause, return to fetch painkillers, swallow two. Already I am aching and ready for a rest. I remember the doctor advising me to 'pace' myself, to schedule regular rests into my diary, but so far today all I have done is pack lunch and put a few things in the car. *I will rest when I get there,* I think, as I ease the car around and set off to the nearest beach, Llanfairfechan, where the sea is reassuringly shallow and if you walk far enough from the car park you can find sand instead of rocks to sit on.

It is brighter now, the temperature gauge on the dash says its already 17°. When we pull up, the seafront it is already busy, and I feel lucky to find a space nearest to where we're heading. We load up ourselves with bags and toys, head across the bridge over the river towards the spot where we will make base camp. Despite the determined sun, the wind here is strong; a warm, raging river of air that makes me eat my hair, whips it into my eyes and mouth, slaps my back. We are buffeted along, smacked sideways, relieved when the pagoda cuts off the assault, our breath stolen when we step out from its protection.

It takes effort to climb over the sea wall and drop onto the warm sand beyond. I spread out a blanket and my son runs in widening arcs as I wriggle my body to create a comfortable recess to lean back into. Here, low behind the curved concrete comfort of the wall, we are protected from the wind. It rushes over our heads and whispers commands at the sand, stirs it into sugar swirls and cinnamon sprinkles. Step away from the wall by just a few metres and it will incite goosebumps to play across your skin.

Tourists are bathing thigh deep in the waves, t-shirts flapping, revealing contours where the wind hugs them. Someone is trying to fly a kite and I realise I meant to bring ours. But memory needs energy or it fails, and this is something else the doctors have argued over.

I have had a number of diagnoses over the years, been bent by physiotherapists and squeezed by rheumatologists. Have given blood and been investigated for Sjorgren's, thyroid issues, rheumatism, liver failure, cancer, auto-immune diseases and anaemia. I've been prescribed ibuprofen, ferric acid, folic acid, diazepam, voltarol, amitriptyline and many other tablets I was reluctant to consume. I've been told I have fibromyalgia, Ehlers-Danlos syndrome, joint hypermobility syndrome, early menopause, hypochondria. I've been told it's stress, pregnancy, normal, imagined.

I've been referred to physiotherapy, to consultants, to hydrotherapy, to an exercise programme to strengthen my core. I've been told to take it easy, to work harder, to find and fund complimentary medicines like acupuncture and aromatherapy. I've been asked to keep a food diary, an activity diary, a mood diary. I've been encouraged to give up work and apply for benefits, to battle through and ignore the cycles of pain and fatigue, to think positive and overcome it by attitude, to go vegan, to eat red meat, to try the 5:2 diet, to exercise more despite the tears in my eyes when I try to walk some days. I've been told it's my own fault, it's hereditary, it's controllable, it's incurable, it's my lifestyle, it's degenerative, it's all in my head. A state of mind.

I've been told I don't *look* like I'm in pain.

I've been told to *smile*. (It might never happen).

I've been told they don't know.

The one thing I do know is it's getting worse, and others in my family are already prisoners to it, already housebound, in wheelchairs. I won't give in – not yet. I want to do as much as possible before I can't do anything. I want to sit in the sand and feel the breeze carry the scent of drying seaweed and fish and chips into my face. But more than that, I want to play football and build a sandcastle with my son. I want to outrun the wind, feel it whip my hair into knots and steal my voice when I shout. I want to be borne by the breeze, suck it into my aching lungs and feel its power surge through me, the oxygen flooding my muscles and organs, feeding every cell. I want to soak up its energy and fly like the sobbing seagulls that are torn through the sky only to land and take off again for another spin.

So I sit, muster the power to play.

From where I am hunkered I can just see the off-shore wind farm further up the coast, the white stalks and thin petals of each turbine shimmer through the rising heat, interrupting the blend of grey and silver where sky and sea meet. Despite the force of the wind, some are still, the blades not turning.

The coast between Ynys Môn and Ellesmere Port is full of them, an advancing alien army dividing the loyalties of the landlubbers and seafarers alike. Like their onshore cousins, they change the landscape, bringing new shapes and sounds to places that pretend they haven't changed in generations, that insist they are still ancient, now violated by technology. The energy companies negotiated deals with farmers with unused land and built thudding white colonies that rise out of the fields in futuristic defiance of the locals. The local and national government are trying to ensure they meet their renewable energy targets, trying to appease the desire for cheap electricity and balance it with the 'not in my backyard' stalwarts who don't mind the entrenched ugliness of concrete buildings or the convenience of a new supermarket, but baulk at how the sea view above the repetitive white blocks of the caravan parks might change. Once you are used to certain shapes and rhythms, to have it changed is traumatic.

Few seem to want them nearby. There are still home-made signs, painted on plywood and speared into garden lawns, declaring *NO* in red. The white pictures of the turbines slashed in blood coloured defiance.

Yet here they are, now so familiar to most that the frustration and resistance must have faded. But anger is an energy too. Maybe somewhere, someone still burns inside at the sight of those slow-spinning spears, their TV on low behind them as they glare through their own reflection at the atrocities they perceive to be lowering their house value.

(I love them).

Like the threaded network of power lines and pylons that hold hands across the mountains and waters, they have become a part of the landscape; familiar and solid. They speak to me of hope, of aspiration, of the human desire to attempt to put things right.

While a part of me romanticises the idea of an energy lock down, a three-day week and a return to growing our own vegetables and trading eggs at the garden gate, I still want to slump into the sofa cushions every night and watch the television. I still want to boil the kettle in minutes and cook when I feel like it without lighting a fire and hanging a pot over it.

I'm hypocritically happy to betray my ancestors and enjoy the modern comforts I'm used to.

(I think I love them).

When I drive past the terrifying heights of the onshore turbines, I can hear and feel the *lub, lub, lub* of their blades like a new heartbeat in the land. They make me feel small and humble, animal. I am vulnerable because I need them while not understanding how they work or if they'll make a difference.

(I'm afraid of them).

I fear they will blow over, I fear they kill birds with their massive spinning blades, that the earth beneath will vibrate a message to the creatures that live there that tells them to flee. I fear the process of installing them in the sea, the resonance of the drilling and piling echoing through the waves, harming marine life. I fear they will not solve the problem of affordable energy and will one day be left for the earth to reclaim, giant rusting monoliths telling the history of hope to future generations.

If we last that long.

I could watch the steady turn of the blades for hours as they translate wind into electricity, one energy into another, a gale into a spark of light on a screen.

(I think I have to love them because they are trying).

At least they are trying.

I stand on the sand and stretch. Spread my arms up and wide in salute to their effort, their steady embrace of the wind that gives them meaning. I parody their motion, feel the breeze strengthen as I step away from the shelter of the sea wall, the sun-hot sand burning my feet, the goosebumps kissed onto my arms with the heady breath of the sky.

I walk faster, wheeling my arms around, spinning a trajectory, feeling the wind push me, shove me, power me forward.

I have caught it: a moment of sheer energy, buoyed and blustered onwards towards the frothy tops of the waves.

My son looks up, eyes scrunched in the slanting sunlight, watching me whirl towards the waves, laughing.

He drops his spade and digger, stands to see me step into the cold water, gasp and step again. Then he runs to me, arms flailing wide, his face a wide grin of delight. As he comes closer, I drop my arms and reach forward, and he's there, a solid weight on my joints. I grasp him and spin, kicking water in freezing fountains up my skirt and legs, turning faster as he squeals at the sheer primal power of it, the force of motion pulling his legs up and out, the strength in my arms as I grip him. The safety of the tight hug to come, when I lower him into the sea and press his face again my stomach so he can't see the pain from the effort of lifting him.

We spin in the wind, and it steals our laughter and takes it away to the turbines to be made into electricity.

TIDAL POWER

We are surrounded by water. In the middle of the summer holidays, there is a deluge that brings relief to the gardens and forests, giving us an excuse to stay in and drink tea, to rest in front of the TV, to read a book. When we do have to leave the house, we fumble for our coats, pull them out from behind the lighter summer wraps, overheating before we arrive anywhere because it isn't cold enough to need their thickness.

Then it's over and the sun returns.

Living by the sea, the water is a backdrop to daily routine. I drive past beaches and the perfect line of the horizon where the water meets the sky, see the colours change hour by hour, day by day, and barely register its existence. There are lakes here, too, and rivers intersecting any journey we make; to walk the dog or drive to the supermarket we rely on bridges that lead us over their fluctuating heights. In the winter the low fields become waterlogged, and the sheep are rescued by the fire service. In the summer, tourists gather on the water edges, some braver than others, stepping deeper or leaping in.

I have never swum in the sea here, or in a lake. Have paddled only rarely. The proximity of the beach somehow destroys the desire. We can go any day, so most days we don't.

But time is running out, and life is short. This summer I need the water. It is primal. I feel dehydrated inside; hollowed out and dry.

The sea will heal me. The lakes and rivers feed my body.

I am scared, though. Scared of the sea's movements and contents, of its risks. I am no swimmer, and I don't understand tides. And the lakes are black and cold and dangerous, the river ready to whip my legs from under me and pull me away, churn me onto rocks and smash my skull, fill my lungs with brackish water.

My friends are not so timid.

One hot day they invite us to Traeth Llanddwyn. I buy a body board for my son as I know the other children will have them. He has a wet suit. I put a bathing suit on under a cotton dress and hope it's not too cold.

When we get to the beach their van is loaded with rubber rings and ropes, a surfboard and wetsuits, fins and goggles. I follow their brown limbs and blonde heads towards the sea and vow to let them lead me on a voyage, desperate to feel the raw energy of the waves and to master my fears of being swept away, of being out of my depth.

We attach body boards to the children's wrists, and rules are laid out before we rush forwards. I am the only one without the protective skin of a wetsuit, I am exposed to the sun and jellyfish, feet bare to weaver fish and their thorny spines. I ignore the voices in my head telling me to watch from the shore, and follow anyway, leaping into the shallows and letting the water lift me, feeling it rock me. The sun makes it warm, its rays filtering through the water and penetrating my skin.

I swim away from the group, confident my son is safely attached to the line of rubber rings and that the other adults are better equipped to ensure his safety than I am anyway. They are taking it in turns to jump from the board. The children fearless in their arm swirling balance and the water's welcoming grasp. They rise and splutter fountains into the sun, faces bobbing like buoys, bright and tethered.

Facing away from the land, I let myself drift, the saline support of the sea sustaining me, cradling me, displaying me for dissection by the sun above. I try not to think of the things living in the deeper waters, the steep drop of sloping land into dark blue danger, the currents and tides that could steal me. I let myself drift and be a part of it, the movement of the water and myself within it, both alien and natural, a motion that I have only ever watched from the shore coursing through me, into me, around me – a wave of energy.

I am hooked. The savoury taste on my lips hours afterwards, the tangle of salt-encrusted hair around my face, the sand that sits between my toes. These things all tell me I have evolved. I am turning into something other, something I never thought possible. I am getting younger, stronger, braver. I long to swim deeper and below the surface, to gain the confidence of a mermaid. I will my body to make serpentine shapes, to shimmer and twist and flex like a fish, like a dolphin. In the water, I am weightless and mobile.

A week later I buy a wet suit and my own board, don't even wait for the hottest days, just take the chance to escape to the coast, any beach where I know the sand slopes slowly, to feel that frightening loss of power the sea provides.

I am careful. Never go in deeper than my waist, knowing that when I'm horizontal in the waves the depth doesn't matter, that when I am thrown towards the beach and my knees scrape on the sand that I am safe, that succumbing was an illusion.

Once I have the added warmth of a wetsuit, we try out the lakes and rivers too, always with the same family; their confidence infectious, their skills reassuring. I stay in the shallows, only watch when they jump off the pontoon into the dark, heartless water of Llanberis lake. We swim in the lagoons, spitting brown water and clinging to low hanging branches for rest when we are tired. I can pretend I am swimming when I am actually just floating, the thick layer of rubber acting as a buoyancy aid, the smallest amount of effort to move through water. When I emerge my weight assails me, surprises me, makes me want to drop to my knees and weep and crawl with all the grace of driftwood. In the water I weigh nothing, my joints at rest, the power of the tide or current does all the hard work. Afterwards, on land, I am grounded, slow and ungainly.

In the river near Beddgelert, we celebrate a birthday. The children play water rescue in a wide, slow section of the river, shouting for help and throwing ropes, enjoying the rush of risk. The adults shiver at the edge. I swim, feeling myself pushed by the flow of water, vulnerable to rocks. Where the water eddies through tight boulders, there is a flume. The children ride it, squealing. I attempt to swim upstream, going nowhere, thinking of salmon. I would let my species die out if that were the only option of procreation.

It's not until we are walking back to the car that I realise how anxious I was in the water. The sea never makes me feel this way.

Near the end of summer we are invited to go surfing properly, a free lesson to learn new skills. We make a day of it, taking body boards out in the morning, despite the clouds that scud above and the wind whipping the water to white tops. I go in with the kids and feel them pulled sideways by the slant of the sand, the turn of the tide. We twist the boards into the rising white waves, power kick to leap and skid above the chilly crystals. When we look, we are two hundred meters away from where we entered the water. I stay between the open sea and my child, grab at his cold hands, feel them dragged away by the force of the next wave. He laughs and turns back towards open water, thrilled with the motion.

We wrestle the waves, struggle with the boards. They are ganging up on us, the wind and sea, trying to call us, drag us, force us back into the water, where together they will separate us from the earth and each other.

Afterwards, we shiver behind a windbreak and eat sandwiches to restore our energy, then walk back to the car to drop off the bags.

Before the proper lesson we are fitted with full length wet suits at the surf shop, walk catlike and sleek through the village of Rhosneigr to the other beach as the sun emerges and illuminates the flat sands in innocent yellow. The sea is calm here, smiling a bay-wide smile, each soft wave tipped with gold. I take a heavy board from the back of the van and try to walk through the water, copy the instructions of the teenage boy for whom the sea is a way of life. He looks like he was born in the waves, sun-bleached and wind-tanned, lithe as a leopard shark. He demonstrates the turns and flips we must emulate to balance on the board, tells us how to read the oncoming waves, when to jump into a standing position. The kids pick it up quick, the adults flounder.

I am so tired halfway through the lesson my legs stop working. I try to crouch and leap, but my toes drag, and I fall into the waves, haul myself back on the board like an injured seal.

In the end I just lie on the board and let the water lift and propel me forwards. I give in to its power, let myself be lulled. It's inside me, all over me, and tastes wonderful. There is no danger here, not now that the sky has brightened and we are surrounded by people who read the sea as easily as I read the faces of my family.

When I peel off the black skin of the wetsuit and start to towel down salt-sore skin, I know I want to come again. I've already forgotten the fear of the sea's cold grasp, its subtle shifting, dragging us away from the safety of shore. I let the sun dry my knotted hair and think of the energy surrounding the island, the persistent surge and retreat of the water, the winter waves crashing over the walls and against the windows of the beach houses.

I have been seduced. The sea is lying to me. It can do what it wants, and we can only pretend we have control.

At the end of summer, the newspapers tell of a boy swept away not far from where we played that day. One big wave and he vanished, his hand yanked away from his grandfather's outstretched grasp by a hungry force with no conscience. Every year there are losses, lifeboats and the coastguard busy all summer, the air-sea rescue helicopters winching people to safety from boats and buoyancy aids.

This summer I think we'll get away with it. I think the good weather has made it safer. I think the dangerous tourist season will soon be over. Then I read the news reports and choke when I discover the lost boy's brother has the same name as my son. I feel ashamed when I realise this coincidence brings me closer, makes it hurt more, when before I'd have only the sorrow of a bystander. I carry his loss like a stone in my chest, unable to stop thinking of his mother's everlasting agony, his father's helplessness, his grandfather's empty hand. The pain will ripple from the photo in the paper like a drop of water in a still lake. The search goes on for weeks. They don't find him.

After the day spent surfing, I lie in bed and try to rest, my arms and legs heavy from gravity's claim on my mass. With the light off and my head pressed deep into the pillow, I can hear the sea whispering in my ear.

I lie still but I'm still moving.

My inner ear is in on the conspiracy, like I am still riding the board, like the bed is lifting and surging forward in moon-guided motion, regular and insistent.

I relent. I imagine the waves and the sun, ride the board again as I drift away, give in to its overriding power.

Nuclear Power

Summer is a social time. Children off school, families booking leave from work, the weather encouraging people to come together outside, make the most it. We are inundated with family wanting to visit, with friends who suddenly have time to speak about more than routine and duty, who want to stay up late and share ideas that will fade as soon as autumn curls the leaves and winter's hood is close to being raised against the cold.

With so many demands on my time and energy, I hide the tiredness and pain behind a bright smile and makeup. Keep it invisible.

We meet up with people at local fairs and festivals, driving across Anglesey on a latticework of roads, always accompanied by the overhead power lines that web the island with silver cables and march, holding hands, across the Menai Straits and away over the mountains.

I barely noticed them before, their height and delicate lace-trestle dresses so much a part of the landscape we inhabit. This summer there are meetings about the new power station; about the benefits and costs of accommodating Wylfa B on land that used to feed cows and sheep, that bathes in ultraviolet radiation all summer and bears the sharp shoulder of cold from the North in winter. There will be new lines installed, their threads trailing over one of three or four proposed routes, and no one is happy with any of them. I am aware and alert for the first time to the invisible energies and threats coursing through the ground and over our heads.

I used to walk my dog past the power lines that draped from pylons rooted in fields by my house, the only ones close enough to notice. In the moist heat of summer they vibrate, a low hum or buzz to rival the sound of insects in the hedgerows either side of the narrow lane. I imagine them snapping, pouring their power straight into the earth, creating a live pool of pain around the feet of the pylons that fizz with static and fry anything that enters.

When the wind blew I would avoid that route for fear of hearing the whipping ping as they broke their chains. I couldn't imagine choosing a house near those dizzying heights, feel the low hum of a headache after standing nearby for too long.

Now I watch the skies and see their spider-silk lines threaded above every horizon. They reveal themselves in their complex webwork and are no longer invisible, unlike the energy that beats from the core of their mother ship.

Wylfa sits like a concrete heart on the edge of the island. Welcomes folk in with its café and visitors centre, its school trips and the beautiful curve of Bae Cemaes behind. It pulsed power through thick veins, feeding the muscle of the National Grid. I avoided the power station in the past, saw enough pictures of its Ukrainian cousin on the television to fear its potential for disaster.

Until I was sent there by my company to work for the day. I had to follow the trail of power lines home to their source, had to confront the low hulk of the concrete building and work its proximity for a day. Over those nine hours, in the company of the men and women who managed the temperatures and mechanics inside its square grey shell, it lost its power over me.

This summer I am drawn back by the debate, want to get closer than before, beyond the visitor's centre and into the core of the building, where the people I meet walk and work and talk to each other, where their energies create energies.

But it's not going to happen.

Since 9/11 the security is fierce, regardless of motive. I settle for watching it at a distance, for noticing the currents and tendrils that surge into the community, both visible and invisible.

Underneath the ground I walk on there are myriad lines and pipes, delivering, removing, transmitting everything we need, or think we need. The power lines above are stitching us together, ensuring we can communicate and learn, that we can achieve and earn.

I think of the chaos even a short power outage creates. Below our bare feet, the cushion of parched grass under our soles, a million living things eat and crawl and shit and procreate. Cycles that are never seen. Among them, cables connect computers with broadband, gas pipes deliver heat, and sewage pipes remove the most natural waste a human can create. We don't want to see that. These things

37

must be hidden, buried like the radioactive waste from the plant; sealed away and only dealt with by men in protective suits, in marked vans. No one really wants to confront the workings of a system, to see the damage of a burst pipe or a crushed cable. We are inconvenienced by the failures.

When 'is everything okay?' is asked, we all expect to the answer to be 'yes, fine.'

Keep the digging to the men in boiler suits and masks. Don't ask too many questions – you might get an answer.

The power lines rise above us, defiant and beautiful. They withstand the wind and sun and ice, and when they fail, we are angry, frustrated by the time it takes to fix the system.

Fearful of the consequences.

Afraid of the dark.

They stand above us and can't be hidden, remind us daily of our desire for electricity, for the convenience and entertainment it provides.

If we care to look.

And they move.

Or rather, if we look as we move, their black silken lines against the startling blue sky or the grey clotted clouds glide against one another in abstract patterns, creating squares and diamonds; hashtags and pie crusts, crosswords and musical scores. Birds sit like notes on the wires, a muted song of symbiosis.

As I trudge through fields towards the latest Wildlife Trust funded festival in the wake of my child, lifting heavy legs to conquer uneven ground, trying not avoid treading on butterflies and spiders, the pylons rise beside me as companions. Urging me onwards, surging with energy. When I meet my friends, I can see the Eifel Tower tessellations reflected in their eyes, know they are invisible to the person whose pupils hold the image, but am reminded to smile, to nod a 'yes, I'm fine thanks' when I'm asked how I'm doing. I know the routine, can keep my secrets as well as the earth holds its own.

I feel the ground trembling with energy beneath me. The worms tunnelling, the rabbits burrowing, the moles digging, the beetles feasting. I need to lie down.

Instead I walk beside striding brown limbs, pretend it doesn't hurt my ghost white legs. I look longingly at the linked arms of the pylons, wishing I could join them, feel the pure electricity surge through me and fill me.

Further along the road, nuclear fission is creating heat, unseen energy that steam-churns the turbines and pours power into the community. If anything goes wrong, we won't see a thing, just like you can't see ultraviolet radiation. The poison that could sap your strength if it leaks from the plant is stealthy, silent, and invisible. Radiation is all around us, in our luminous watches and the sun and the bananas we eat when we stop to sit on a hay bale beside the track. Anything could happen – we could make history if things went wrong.

In the evenings we cook, turn the radio up to feel the music beat a rhythm to move to, settle down to watch the television or read by the lamp's artificial glare.

I am recharging, letting the comfort of convenience give me rest. Like everyone else I can close my eyes and not see the wires that string above us. I don't know what will be decided, what route the new lines will take, or even if a new power station will actually appear to change the landscape with its shadow.

Right now I have to smile and say I'm fine, keep things invisible, a threat without shape or warning.

FOSSIL FUEL

The chimney pots are laughing. Or rather, the jackdaws nesting in them are. A *chack chack* chuckle that always makes me smile.

Although the cool chills of spring have faded, we still want to light the fire some nights just to sit and feel its warm fingers of light play over our faces. But the smoke is returning, pouring inwards and filling the room with a cloud of black velvet dust that I'm still wiping off the shelves a month later. We quickly pour water into the hearth, its fizzing hiss belching yellow smoke that smells of sulphur and hell and everything we should fear. We cough and splutter, pull cardigans tighter, listen to the cosy jackdaws tell us jokes from the network of chimneys above us.

We have four pots on the roof, cracked terracotta leading to four fireplaces, two of which have been erased completely leaving blank walls where a hearth should be, and one concreted up, leaving a blinded ceramic fire-surround and mantelpiece. Only fireplace is open: our primary source of warmth and hot water in the winter to come.

We burn prehistoric forests in carbon coal cobbles that glow like dragon eggs in the hearth. We burn spitting logs, the woodsmoke giving the room a medieval scent.

We sometimes toast crumpets and bread sitting around this age-old energy source, warming our hands in its soft orange light. I feel connected beside the fire, at rest in more than body.

When we split the logs, raising the heavy axe with weary arms, the thud and clink of the blade kissing wood, hitting the concrete beneath, we are fulfilling something deep inside, and the ache in the arms that follows is a sweet memory of who we should be.

We've been mocked for not installing gas central heating, for not having a thermostat we can ignore, warm mornings to ease us into the day. Right now we don't think about the prospect of ice on the inside of the windows, the dragon breath we'll billow out on cold winter mornings. It's warm outside and we don't really need the fire right now.

We wait for the jackdaws to fledge. I'm woken every day by the chicks' greedy calls to their parents and the scratching of their claws in the chimney beside the bed. I'm warmed by the knowledge that another generation of grey-hooded, white-eyed comedians is flourishing inside my house.

We keep the patio doors open, let the sun warm the room, listen to the birds in the trees argue over the flies and bugs. The fireplace can stay silent, the ash a soft layer of grey over the grate. Once the soot-black baby birds emerge, their moon-pale eyes searching the horizon, rising like puffs of smoke from the warm, round pot, we'll cap the chimney. We'll remove their lattice work of sticks so the smoke can rise and not choke us. We'll evict the jackdaws with enough time over the summer for them to find a new hole. We hope they'll move to the next pot along, nest in the redundant tunnels that will still be warmed by the house, keeping the chill off their midnight wings.

For now we sit beside the open mouth of the cold fireplace and listen to this corvid family telling jokes to their children. The babies chuckle in delight. We don't need the fire yet and my joints are glad, enjoy the respite from hauling coal and chopping logs. Despite the pleasure from that first crackling spark, I need to save my energy, enjoy the rest from chores. Each year the task gets harder, requires longer recuperation. I don't want to give up on the primal pleasure of the feel of fire against my cold skin, but I know one day I'll be relying on a thermostat to heat my bones and get me going in the morning.

This summer we laugh with the jackdaws, throw bread on the flat roof of the shed to feed their ravenous mouths, make the babies fat and strong. We listen to the *chack chack* chuckles growing louder, stronger, and have a little chuckle ourselves.

WILL POWER

Remember me, hanging from the rock?

It's the end of summer and my resources are low. I jumped into the season headfirst this year, desperate to do things I've never thought necessary, never felt the rush to do. The sea has always been there, the mountains aren't moving, the veins of electricity beneath and above us continue to hum, the wind is always waiting to tear through your coat and whisk you away.

This summer, I really needed to feel it. To be in it. To push my hands into the soil, lie flat on the grass, and let the Earth's energy swell up into my muscles, to let the wind steal my breath and return it tenfold, and to feel the sea tug at my fears and roll me back to the shoreline. To look Wylfa in the eye and not back down.

When they asked me to step forward and get fitted for the harness, I could barely stand. My condition, whatever it is, had flared up, aggravated by me ignoring it, pushing myself to go out and explore the island, the mainland, the power in the land. I had already shovelled as many painkillers into my mouth as I could safely take. Had sat down at every opportunity, feeling like my limbs were made of stone. I looked up at the rock face, at the children whizz up and down its stony features, and it seemed ten times higher than I knew it was. I'd already given up my place in the queue once, gifting a little girl the chance to test her developing limbs on another plane.

But there was the man holding out the helmet, shaking the

harness, smiling at me. He could see, behind the mask of pain and the frown of exhaustion, that there was a little girl in me shouting *Come on! When are you going to get the chance to engage so completely with these mountains again? Next year you'll be older, even more tired. This could be it! Get off your backside and get up there!*

So I got up.

The crack of my knees was like wood spitting in fire as I straightened and stepped forward. My legs slid into the thick straps of the harness and the helmet tightened around my head.

I met my son's steady stare, his triumph of conquering the wall still glowing in his cheeks, his expectation of my achievement burning in his eyes.

I looked at the person belaying, tried to calculate our contrasting body mass. If I let go, slip or lose my grip, would I plummet while he rose? Would I smash to the earth like a conker? Lose my mobility in one fell swoop instead of through years of degeneration?

He reassured me, pointed to the first foothold, smiled. Couldn't see the effort it took to step forward, can't understand how much harder this climb would be for me than for the fizzing balls of energy that chatter to their parents behind me.

Are you okay? he asked.

I'm fine.

Kept my smile fixed, kept the pain invisible. Gripped the first crevice with fear-slicked fingers and hauled myself up. Each stretch and grasp drawing glucose from my blood, adrenalin surging, masking pain.

I looked up, saw the knotted rope I have to reach, the bell a burnished curve in dying light. I could feel the eyes of my son and husband like an energy boost.

I kept going, my heart thumping like a wind turbine, the sway of my body rocking gently like the tide. Harnessed every memory that the earth had given me over the last few months as I sucked air into exhausted lungs, the oxygen feeding my tissues. The sun on my freckled arms, determination smouldering in my core...

I am close, but not close enough. I stop and look at the line of rope rising six more feet above me.

I'm done.

Here I am, clinging on.

I'm lichen, I'm moss, I'm the trembling tree rooted in the memory of soil beside me.

And I'm tired.

I want to give up, to be slowly lowered back to solid ground and the supportive arm of my husband, to go home, to lie on the sofa, to rest.

I look down and see my son's face, small and round, pale as a jackdaw's eye against the black slate path. His voice is distant, dizzying. He knows I can do it because I can do anything. That's what parents do. He claps, and it sounds like thunder.

I turn back and hug the stone, ignore the man belaying for me who asks if I want to come down. I force another stretch from an aching arm. There is no adrenaline left.

I'm using borrowed energy. I'm sucking power from the rock itself. I'm not going down until I've touched the knotted rope at the top, rung that bell. I ignore the lactic acid in my thighs and push on. I feel the sun burning the back of my neck and reach higher. My teeth are aching from the pressure my jaws exert.

One last stretch.

The rope knot is rough in my sweat-slicked fingers. I cling to it and turn, wave a shaking arm at my miniature family. Let out a breath that shudders in my chest as it is released.

The bell chimes, a public accomplishment.

No one sees me kiss the rock or whisper a prayer of thanks into the breeze. I am filled with gratitude for the world around me, for the trees and soil and stone and sun and water and wind that led me here.

I know I'll never do this again; the only thing I'll take away is the increased throb of pain in my joints and a need to sleep longer than usual tonight.

And the memory. The knowledge that today, at least, my willpower was enough.

I descend. It takes only a few moments and my ears pop about halfway down. Little arms encircle my waist, and a big hand takes my own, steadies my steps over the loose rocks at the bottom. I step out of the harness and hand back the helmet. Summer is over.

I did it.

And that's enough for now.

Notes and Acknowledgements

This memoir was Highly Commended in the 2015 New Welsh Writing Awards, and an extract published in the New Welsh Reader #108. All references to places and events are from the summer of 2014.

Thanks, always, to my husband and son for their unending support in a million ways, and to all the friends and family who appear in here as part of this tiny slice of my life. To the team at the New Welsh Review for supporting this mini-memoir, and to the team at Broken Sleep Books, you are a joy and inspiration to work with. To write openly about disability, to acknowledge it so publicly, is not easy, but it is necessary, and made possible by the support and commitment of BSB to diversity and equality.

LAY OUT YOUR UNREST

www.ingramcontent.com/pod-product-compliance
Lightning Source LLC
Chambersburg PA
CBHW021337290326
41933CB00038B/957